Copyright © M L Hol[...]
Theory.

The right of M L Holde[...] author of this work has [...] accordance with the copyright, Designs and Patents Act 1988.

The 'So What!' Theory is a registered trademark. All rights reserved. This book or any portion thereof may not be reproduced or used in any manner whatsoever without the express written permission of the author except for the use of brief quotations in a book review

The 'So What!' Theory

M L Holder

DEDICATION

This book is dedicated to my amazing husband Mike and our beautiful children Chris and Lea – you are my world and my inspiration. You remind me of the beauty in humanity on a daily basis. I love you all to the moon and back..."*Anything is possible when you're happy!*"

"Hold onto the positive things in your life – if you can't see them, lift the veil that surrounds them, because they are there. Sometimes you just have to look closer"
  M L HOLDER –THE 'SO WHAT!' THEORY

PAGE NUMBERS

2	ACKNOWLEDGEMENTS
3	A NOTE FROM THE AUTHOR
8	INTRODUCTION
12	THE THEORY
29	EXAMPLES
77	EXERCISES
83	SELF HELP

1   ACKNOWLEDGEMENTS

There are so many people in my life that have made my own life journey a positive one. My Family are naturally the top of this list! They have always been there for me whenever I have needed them, and I feel truly blessed to have them in my life. I've been lucky enough to have worked with some amazing people, but a special mention must go to Jacqui, Maddy and Corinne. You always bring me tears of joy - we truly have had some fun times together! I want to thank Penni for reminding me of my own positive outlook at a time when I nearly lost my way. I want to thank Fi and Clare and the countless friends and family members who kindly visited me at the worst time of my life – their kindness has never been forgotten. And finally my soul sisters Tink and Hilary, who encouraged me to continue what I had already started and who reminded me that this book would help and inspire others.

2   A NOTE FROM THE AUTHOR

"We all have mountains to climb, some of us immediately head straight to the top!"
M L Holder THE 'SO WHAT!' THEORY

This book is written for everyone. From those who live positive lives and are looking for ways to boost this further, to those that have occasional negative thoughts and want to find a simple way to stop this from happing or escalating. It is also perfect for those who recognise that much of their thinking is pessimistic and want to change their whole outlook on life and effect major change for the positive.

Throughout my life I have always had a fairly positive outlook. Things never seemed to get me down in the same way as it did others. I think I had a more natural positive way of viewing the world I lived in. I still had the same issues growing up as every other child did, but would often find I could perhaps cope better than others. I didn't grow up in a constantly happy 'bubble', there were plenty of times when my home-life was, admittedly, quite negative for me – however, I somehow managed to get by with a smile. I naturally sought the positive in people and often felt that life could be so much better if people wanted it to be. I grew up with the ability to 'sense' the mood of a room, I would know to avoid certain people and was always attracted towards happy people. Clearly back then I had the ability to feel negative and positive energy!

Below are the words of a song by Jerome Kern and Dorothy Fields – I remember hearing them as a young child when watching the movie 'Swing Time' with Fred Astaire and Ginger Rogers, and thinking what lovely words they were. It was also a popular song, when later recorded by Nat King Cole. Some of the words have stuck with me through life and just about sum up what I'm like when something happens to me personally! I do 'pick myself up' and 'dust myself off' and 'start all over again'.

Pick yourself up….
Take a deep breath
Dust yourself off
And start all over again

Nothing's impossible, I have found

For when my chin is on the ground.
I pick myself up,
Dust myself off
And start all over again.

Don't lose your confidence
If you slip
Be grateful for a pleasant trip
And pick yourself up,
Dust yourself off
And start all over again.

Work like a soul inspired
Until the battle of the day is won.
You may be sick and tired,
But you'll be a man my son.

Will you remember the famous men
Who had to fall and rise again?
They picked themselves up
Dusted themselves off
And started all over again.

The universe has always supported me and given me everything I ever needed and I am always grateful for this. Today I believe and know that the universe will always provide me with anything I want as well. I know beyond any doubt that if I visualise, believe, feel and give thanks of gratitude, I will receive what I want. It truly is a wonderful knowledge to have. All my thoughts are energy, I am energy, and my feelings are too.

I wanted to write an amazing book based on something I myself call The 'So What!' Theory. I want to help people around this planet of ours to be able to understand and apply this theory, which encompasses Universal Law, to their daily lives. I want to inspire others and help them through their own spiritual journey.

This book is written in simple, understandable terms, so the reader can easily relate to it and effectively apply it in their own way, for the benefit of all. My vision is that The 'So What!' Theory will reach a worldwide audience and very quickly become so well known that people will be saying 'So What!' and applying its principles on a daily basis. These words will act as a trigger to remind the reader to change their thinking into positive thoughts anytime and anywhere. This book will enable so much good to be achieved by everyone who reads it! The book is supported by The 'So What!' Theory website www.thesowhattheory.com which aims to help the reader to continue to apply the theory and stay positive. There is also a Facebook page with uplifting quotes and posters.

Above all, this book is written with love, compassion, honesty, empathy and feeling. It is directed at anyone who wants to change their outlook on life to a positive, happy and confident one. It will give its readers a boost and will help the reader to change their mind-set and ultimately see the positive where previously they only saw negatives. Thank you for reading this book.

"It's the positive things in life that make us happy" M L Holder THE 'SO WHAT!' THEORY

3   INTRODUCTION

We live in a world that is constantly filled with negativity, whether it's from the daily news, social media, the people around us, or even from our own thinking. It surrounds us in our daily lives whether we notice it or not! We may not even realise it – but stop and think about it for a second, we are continually bombarded with negative images, thoughts, news, arguments, issues etc. In addition to this that we are often surrounded by negative emotions, negative energy, negative thinking and without realising it, we pick it up, absorb it, and all too often, we continue its cycle and we pass it on.

Have you ever thought 'I wish I'd handled that situation better' or 'I'm tired of all the negativity surrounding me' or 'wouldn't the world be a better place if we could all get along' or 'I'm angry and frustrated about this situation'…

Have you ever been in a situation and found it physically and mentally draining? Do you want to change how you mentally and physically feel about certain situations? Do you want to feel more positive about life, about work, about relationships, about money, about your health? If the answer is "YES", then this is the perfect book for you!

This book will explain The 'So What!' Theory in a way that everyone can relate to, with easy to follow hints, tips and guides to help you to change the negative to the positive. With real life examples of The 'So What!' Theory in use, it will show how it has been applied and used to turn things around to positive effect. It includes a 'self-help' guide – which will help you to see how easy it is to gain instant results using The 'So What!' Theory. With a selection of simple 'exercises' that you can try, you will quickly be able to turn negative situations and thinking into positive ones! The 'So What!' Theory will enable you to change the way you feel about things, for the better. It will help you to break the cycle of negativity around you by making simple changes using this book as a guide. The 'So What!' Theory will help you to see and feel instant results.

"Small steps are all it takes to start a journey" M L Holder THE 'SO WHAT!' THEORY

The 'So What!' Theory is a way of saying '**So What!**' to a situation and looking at it in a different, more positive way. It is a simple, effective technique to help you change any negative thoughts into positive ones. It can be quickly and easily applied anywhere at any time.

Many people throughout my life, have often asked me how I stay so positive when times are tough. They are intrigued as to why I am always happy, smiling and content. It's because I apply "The 'So What!' Theory" all the time! It works for me – it can work for you. You just need to give it a try. It's that simple! Of course everyone, including me, has had negative thoughts about a situation. We are, after all, human and its human nature to have varying thoughts and feelings. What this book does, is it highlights or flags up the fact that when you do have a negative thought, you can change it.

Throughout the book, bolded letters will act as a visual aid to **positive** thinking. By the time you have finished reading this book you will easily be able to:

- Apply The 'So What!' Theory to effect change for the **good** in your life.

- Use The 'So What!' Theory as a way to **de-stress** your life, quickly and simply!

- Let The 'So What!' Theory become part of your everyday life and change your outlook from negative to **positive**!

- Acknowledge that The 'So What!' Theory is for everyone and is **easy** to follow. Not only that, you **can** help others to make changes to their lives - your children, partner, colleagues, friends – literally anyone.

- Let The 'So What!' Theory help you to leave negative thoughts in the past and start this day as a new **positive** day and every day moving forward.

- Remember- you **can** do this!

"Change your thinking today, and change your life forever"...THE 'SO WHAT!' THEORY

4   THE THEORY

So, what is my theory?!

The 'So What!' Theory is a new approach to thinking that anyone and everyone can follow. It looks at how we can change our negative thoughts into positive thoughts quickly and this can actually make our lives better, **happier**, healthier and enriched.

It is my belief that we are not born negative, unhappy, prejudiced or stressed! These thoughts and emotions arise from external influences that we experience or are taught throughout our lives. I feel we owe it to ourselves to be happy positive human beings that are able to lead **contented** lives with a positive frame of mind. No-one can give this to us – we lead our own pathway through life, we have 'free will' to choose our own thoughts and destination. I hope to remind the reader through this book, that they too deserve to live a positive way of life that is both enjoyable and fruitful. The 'So What!' Theory has evolved to help achieve this.

"Good things do happen – you just need to believe it!" M L Holder THE 'SO WHAT!' THEORY

Of course changing the way we think is nothing new – there have been many phrases used over time that have the same uplifting message. Many of these you will have heard before!

- Keep your chin up
- Put your best foot forward
- Have a positive mental attitude
- My glass is 'half full'
- Keep on keeping on
- You can achieve anything if you put your mind to it
- What you sow, so you shall reap
- Don't bring me problems, bring me solutions
- Happiness is a state of mind

It is important here to understand the meaning of negativity and positivity before we can apply The 'So What!' Theory to make the changes we need to.

What is negativity? Negative can be a thought or an emotion, it can mean a refusal to accept something or a situation. It can be an attitude, a frame of mind and a form of resistance or disinterest. Someone who is negative can be disagreeable or lacking in enthusiasm. A negative person can be seen as pessimistic, unhappy or in denial. We can all think of negative words and sayings. However I have deliberately chosen not to provide a list of these words within this book, as I don't want to attract any negative thinking and evoke negative feelings by allowing you, the reader to focus on this!

What is positivity? Positive can also be a thought or an emotion. Positivity can be seen as something good, great, and brilliant that makes someone happy, smiling, agreeable, **enthusiastic** and excited. I have included as many positive words and phrases as I can throughout this book. There is also a page at the back of this book dedicated to positive words specifically called The 'Page of Positivity'. Use these words whenever you need to, as a visual aid to help you change your thinking at any time and to remind yourself what being positive is!

Cut out the page and use it to help you when you need to think of a positive word or cut them out and stick them in places you feel would help! If you always have a bad day at the desk, cut positive words out and stick them around your workspace. It will really help to lift your mood. There is also a downloadable version on the website www.thesowhattheory.com

"You can't live your life in a positive way if you are constantly thinking negatively" M L Holder THE 'SO WHAT!' THEORY

The 'So What!' Theory may just be that new approach to thinking that you are seeking – one that will help you to make changes to your own life as well as one than can help others around you to make changes - your children, partner, colleagues, siblings, friends. Literally anyone in and around your life.

"Leave negative thoughts in the past, start this day as a new positive day and every day moving forward" M L Holder THE 'SO WHAT!' THEORY

The 'So What!' Theory can be used in any situation and is based on the theory that you can change the way you are thinking at any particular given moment. It acts as a visual and mental reminder to stop the current way you are thinking and to change it. It encourages the user to put a mental hold onto a negative thought and to re-assess that thought and apply a **positive** spin on it, thus changing your thinking about the situation, your feelings about it and ultimately changing your reaction to something.

Everything in the universe has its own energy. We are made up of energy, animals are, plants and trees are too, and energy has an effect on us. As humans, our physical being is made up of cells and each cell is made of vibrations of energy. Not only are our bodies made up of energy, but our thoughts are too as our minds also emit vibrations of energy.

You may have heard various phraseology such as 'mind over matter' or 'the power of thought'. Our thoughts are powerful, they control our lives even when we are unaware.

A good example of this is when you are told not to picture something and you just do! If I told you NOT to picture a rainbow, I'll bet the first thing you thought of WAS a rainbow! In the same way if I told you to think of someone laughing, really laughing, a **good** belly laugh - it is likely it would brighten your mood and could even make you smile! This also proves that thoughts affect our emotions too. This is a good thing to know, because now you can realise that different thoughts can connect to differing emotions within us. It also shows that we are fully capable of changing our thoughts for the **better**!

Have you ever walked into a room with people that you know are particularly negative, or are arguing and felt a change in the energy in the room – felt drained? This is because we are made up of energy too and we are sensitive to the energy around us. It is common for **happy**, positive people with good energy levels around them to attract others who are the same... you may find when you are in a **great** mood you are attracted towards others who are also in the same mood. Similarly you may find when you are amongst people who are in a negative, angry, frustrated mood, the atmosphere has changed to a negative one – this is because again, you are sensing and absorbing it.

How often do we stop to think about our own thoughts? For most of us I suspect not very often. Yet if we were to assess our thinking more often, particularly in difficult situations or when things are not going well, we may find that we should take more note of something so powerful!

"Listen to your higher self, it is telling you to be happy" M L Holder THE 'SO WHAT!' THEORY

Wouldn't it be **wonderful** if we could, when things are not going so well and we are thinking negatively, stop ourselves from continuing to do so? How great would it be to flip that thinking around and change it to a positive and affect the outcome of the situation for the better! The 'So What!' Theory helps you to do this. It becomes your very own 'Thought "STOP!" Point'. It brings your current thinking into focus and enables you to make the appropriate changes for a **better** outcome.

The same can be said for emotions – these are naturally attached to our thoughts. Change your thoughts and it changes your emotions. It really is that simple. The 'So What!' Theory can also be easily applied as a 'Thought "STOP!" Point' for your emotions too. Using The 'So What!' Theory, you can quickly be back in control of how you want to think and feel. We are unable think negative thoughts and positive thoughts at the same time, just in the same way you can't feel negative and positive emotions at the same time. This book helps to remind you that **you can** think and feel positive, **you can** change your energy, and **you can** bring about change in your life today and every day!

"When life feels like it's letting you down, apply THE 'SO WHAT!' THEORY and turn it

around" M L Holder **THE 'SO WHAT!' THEORY**

I think we can all think of someone in our lives who is always negative. Not only are they always negative, there is always something wrong with them, they complain constantly of issues they have with this and that – they fall out with people easily, nothing ever goes 'right' for them! On the other side, you can probably think of someone in your life that is always cheery, positive, happy, **content** and has little to moan about in their lives. The reason for this is simple – Universal Law, or what is commonly known as the 'Law of Attraction'.

The power of the mind is a **wonderful** thing and if used correctly, it can help us to attract whatever we want into our lives! The Universal Law of Attraction is a simple belief and understanding that 'like attracts like'. By the same token, 'like energy attracts like energy'. An easy way to understand this is through our thought processes – what you send out will come back to you. We are effectively a thinking magnet and what we put out there, we will attract back to us. So sending out good thoughts attracts them back! Using the Law of Attraction helps us to bring into our lives the things that we want. It is important therefore, to focus on **good** things, send positive thoughts and use positive language as often as possible. This is even more important when you realise that we have, on average around 50,000 – 70,000 thoughts per day! So, if you find yourself thinking negative thoughts or having negative feelings, apply The 'So What!' Theory, stop yourself, and get your **positive** thinking back on track again!

"Thoughts are energies, we send them out into the universe. Send good thoughts and attract good thoughts, it's as simple as that" M L Holder THE 'SO WHAT!' THEORY

How does positive energy work and what is it?

If we have positive energy flowing from us, we attract positive energy. If we have negative energy flowing from us, then we will attract negative energy. It's as simple as that! If we think negative thoughts, we attract more of the same – sometimes to such an extent that it creates a downward spiral so that everything in our lives can become so negative that it leaves us feeling hopeless, lost, miserable and extremely unhappy. So if we can think positive thoughts, we will attract positivity into our lives

– **contentment**, happiness, and a brighter outlook on life altogether.

The 'So What!' Theory teaches us to change our thinking bit by bit to help guide us away from the negative energy and the negative thinking into a positive frame of mind whereby we can alter our mental state and the outcome is a good one.

Changing our thoughts is quick and simple – here is an example, give it a try!
Picture in your minds' eye yourself picking up your post from your front doormat and finding three envelopes, all of them you quickly realise are bills to be paid. How does this make you feel? Are you feeling a bit low or frustrated that they've all come at once? Did your shoulders feel like they sagged a little with disappointment? Hold onto that feeling and thought process and remember what it feels like, make a mental note of it...

Now I want you to picture the very same front door – you pick up the three envelopes and open the first letter which is a large cheque for an unexpected refund on a utility bill. (Wow that's great!) The next envelope contains a thank you card from a friend who you helped last week with an issue they had. The card is

beautiful with really lovely words inside and totally unexpected. The third envelope is an invite to a party next week and you are really excited as you haven't been to a party for ages! How are you feeling now? Happy? Excited? Smiling and **uplifted**? Hold onto this feeling and thought process and remember what it feels like...

You will see how different your feelings and your emotions were to both situations. The first was a series of negative thoughts, the second a series of positive ones. Notice how the feelings and emotions got either better or worse as you visualised each situation. Add negative to negative and it makes you feel low, sad, unhappy, miserable and it's easy to spiral downwards from this. Take positive thoughts and feelings, add more and the result is uplifting! The more you add the better the feeling and the better the emotions.

"If you can think positively and feel positively, only positive things can happen!" M L Holder THE 'SO WHAT!' THEORY

All of our thoughts have energy, so these examples show how easily the energy can be changed! Same front door, same three envelopes, but completely different thoughts and emotions attached to the two example situations.

Try a little exercise yourself here and think of a situation you have been through, maybe recently or in the past where it was negative – think about how you felt at the time, what were your emotions like? How did you react? How is that making you feel right now? If it helps, write down your thoughts and emotions.

Next try to think of a situation where it was a positive, something happened that made you happy and **smile**. Again think – how did you feel at the time, what were your emotions like? How is that thought making you feel right now? If it helps, write down your thoughts and emotions.

So you see, just by imagining a specific situation and attaching positive or negative emotions to it can create energy and a feeling inside yourself.

Guess what – you can now apply that process and change the way you think. By changing the way you think, you change the way you feel and you change your emotional attachment to that thought or situation.

By applying The 'So What!' Theory, you can and will **achieve** a better mind set and this will automatically help in any situation. The 'So What!' Theory can literally change your outlook on life, break down the barriers to your thinking and set you free to change your life into one that you want – you can be positive and do the things that you want to do rather than the things you don't want to do! Concentrate on what you want from a situation not what you don't!

Think it, visualise it, feel it, **believe** in it, ask for it, attract it to yourself and then – receive it!

"The power of positive thinking knows no limits" M L Holder THE 'SO WHAT!' THEORY
We are not born with negative thoughts, self-imposed restrictions, we allow our own minds and external influences to do this. Break free from this, attract positive energy, a positive mind and each step you take is a step nearer to a **happier** life. The 'So What!' Theory can be practised in any area of your life successfully. Practise on small things to start with and build it up – change your thinking today! Now!

Not everyone has negative thoughts constantly, of course some do and almost all of us know someone who fits that description. The 'So What!' Theory can help even if it's just the occasional negative thought. Even though it can be done, it's a challenge for anyone to have positive thoughts all day long every day! Have you ever heard that expression "I'm having a bad day, it started off bad this morning and it's just getting worse and worse"? Well, The 'So What!' Theory is there to help you **change** that – it is there to help you turn this kind of day around. Remember like attracts like and so if you stop thinking negative and start thinking positive, positive things happen.

The 'So What!' Theory = turning your negative to positive.

In a bad situation? Stop, think about what's going wrong here... how can you make it better? Change the way you are thinking about the situation, find a positive solution and move forward. Say to yourself 'So What!' I can change this, I can sort this out. Use positive thinking to help you change things.

Always having a bad day at your place of work? Then stop what you are doing, say 'So What!'

apply The 'So What!' Theory and change things – it's in your power to do so, so do it!

We lead busy lives, rushing around, achieving as much as we can in our day with little time to stop and reflect on our thinking, our actions and our emotions. Take some time to think over your life, or even just how your day went today. Were there negatives in your day, were there things you'd like to have gone better? How would you like them to have played out in a perfect day? If you had that day again now, what would you have done differently? Try it now! Is a different day now playing through your mind? – Almost certainly the answer will be yes! (See! it could have been a **great** day) So, the next time you are having a difficult moment in your day apply The 'So What!' Theory. Stop, assess your thinking, put a positive spin on it and change your thinking, then move on.

Does our thinking affect our health? Absolutely yes! How we think has a major effect on our health. Our thinking affects our emotions and this has an effect on our body. Happy and positive emotions make us feel great, wonderful, **amazing**. Negative emotions and thoughts have the opposite effect. Remember we are human magnets and what we put out, we attract back!

Do you stress over things? Even the simplest of things? Sometimes it's the smallest of things that stress us the most in our modern everyday life. Have you ever really considered what stress actually is? If you look in any dictionary for a definition they will all say pretty much the same thing - that stress is a state of mind, it is an emotional strain, tension, worry, anxiety or pressure. Stress can evoke within us negative thoughts, emotions and energy.

Is the stressing helping your situation? I can bet your answer is No! Well then, apply The 'So What!' Theory and change your thinking. Remember The 'So What!' Theory is a reminder to STOP your current thinking, to say 'So What!' and to think of a positive solution. Start to change your thinking and attract positive thoughts and energy. Check the self-help section in this book for ways to help with stress.

The 'So What!' Theory is so simple, it can be applied in any situation from health, relationships, work, money, family or anything you can think of!

"Had a bad day? So What! Make tomorrow a better one" M L Holder THE 'SO WHAT!' THEORY

There will be exercises later in this book for you to try – they will help get you started and once you start practising The 'So What!' Theory more, it will really turn your day around. Before you know it you will have had a **better** week, month and year!

Remember to apply The 'So What!' Theory as often as you can and certainly whenever you have any negative thoughts, wherever they may be.

Use the visual aids in this book and stick them to objects that will help you to remember to think **positively**. E.g. at the desk, cut out a 'So What!' speech bubble and put it somewhere visible as a prompt. At home, stick one on your kitchen cupboard, on the fridge, or even on the mirror you use first thing in the morning. Use it anywhere you know that you may have specific negative thoughts. You can download and print these visual aids from the website.

"Change your thinking <u>today</u>, and change your life <u>forever</u>"...THE 'SO WHAT!' THEORY

5 EXAMPLES

All of these examples are 'real-life' and have happened. Some of them are examples of truly life-changing situations. We all have experiences that affect us in many ways throughout our life and these examples show that no matter how bad a situation can get, there is always a positive to be found. Applying The 'So What!' Theory can and does help to bring about **effective** change to any given situation, anytime and anywhere.

"Step over life's hurdles and onto a clear path with the knowledge that you can succeed" M L Holder THE 'SO WHAT!' THEORY

Example 1.

I knew I was different from everyone else by the time I has half way through my primary school years. I started to notice people looking at me that little bit longer than they did to everyone else. I knew I looked different – every time I looked into the mirror I was reminded of that! My nose was quite badly bent in the middle and the bottom half had sort of grown sideways so that it looked quite strange. Everyone at primary school just treated me normally, a few people made comments but nothing serious. I was very conscious of it though and hated it.

By the time I started secondary school, I was getting bullied because of it. Name calling started and I was being singled out on a daily basis. It didn't help that I was very tall, slim and quiet by nature. By the time I was 12, I think I had heard every derogatory name calling about my nose that there was - 'follow your nose and you'll go round in circles'. 'bent nose girl', 'ugly', 'do you smell round corners', 'clearly you were last in the que when god dished out noses', 'weirdo' and many others too rude to mention here.
I started getting a complex. I was literally the only person that I knew with a bent nose. I had

never seen anyone else with a bent nose like mine! I really stood out being so skinny, so tall and with a bent nose. Not only did it affect my looks, but I couldn't actually breathe properly or smell properly. I started to worry about my future and believed no partner would want to be with me or marry me with a face like this! I couldn't get away from it either – it's in the middle of my face, there is no hiding from that! Surely I was destined to live a life with negative thoughts and emotions surrounding my looks and how people saw me.

I had many 'tough' talks with myself – there was after all, nothing I could do about the situation. I wasn't about to change people's view of me and I couldn't change the appearance of my nose.

So, I made a decision to change the way I thought about my situation. To start to accept myself, to accept my looks and to accept that people were going to react. People who met me for the first time always looked that little bit longer at my face, but said nothing and I knew that this was normal human behaviour and I could do little to change it. I promised myself that I was not going to let this affect how I felt about myself any longer – people could react how they wanted or say what they wanted but I would be fine with that. I would hold my head up high and move on. I slowly started to change my thinking about my nose, my appearance and my outlook. I won't lie, it took time and effort and there were times when I had to 'check myself' and alter my thinking, but the more I did it, the easier it got. I soon realised that it was far more important to know what I personally felt about myself than what others did. After all, I lived with this day in day out, they didn't!

I started to believe I was as good as anyone else, I told myself I was unique rather than different! I told myself that there would be someone out there who would love me as I was. I decided that I was not going to let my facial disfigurement affect my life anymore. From then on, I felt so much happier and could easily brush off any negative comments and thoughts and turn them into positive ones. I remember being about 13 and watching the news on TV and seeing an amputee struggling to get around on one leg and thinking 'I have nothing to complain about do I really? - I only have a bent nose. This person only has one leg – I am the lucky one here. Again and again, I would see news stories of people who were in a far worse situation than myself, so I used this as a mental note. Whenever I felt negative about my appearance, I would think of someone I had seen on the news in a far worse situation than me and remind myself how lucky I was. It helped me immensely because I never looked back. Even when years later, I had an operation to rebuild my nose, only to have it collapse months later, leaving me looking just as bad as when I had started. I still kept positive and thought 'there are people far worse off than me so why complain'. A few years on from this, I had a bone graft from my hip to rebuild the nose again using metal wiring. Even then I refused to complain of the pain, the process, and the lengthy stares. To this day, 30 years on, my nose still looks 'not quite right' but I don't care... there is always, always, someone worse off than me. I have a nose, I can smell, I can be **confident** about who I am, how I look, how I feel about myself – all because I chose not to attach negativity to my thoughts, instead I saw the positives and changed my thinking for the better.

Negative thoughts about yourself and your appearance can lead to anxiety, stress and in some cases paranoia. Things can easily spiral out of control and it can seriously affect your relationship not just with yourself but also with those around you. STOP this negative thinking, apply The 'So What!' Theory and look for the positives – there will be many that you have overlooked! What matters is you and how you feel about yourself. What others think is not important. You are on your own life pathway so focus on that. How would you like to feel about yourself – think about it, write it down, read it through and start to imagine yourself feeling only positive and good things about yourself! **Love** *yourself, be kind to yourself, allow yourself to grow in confidence. You are beautiful and don't let anyone tell you any different. Change your outlook, ignore any negative comments about your appearance. If negative thoughts creep back in, apply The 'So What!' Theory and change your thinking back to positive.*

"Let us help one another to be the very best that we can be" M L Holder THE 'SO WHAT!' THEORY

Example 2.

My job was amazing – well it was a career rather than a job. I saw myself working through to retirement in this particular role. I loved it, it paid really well and I had great colleagues, a lot of flexibility in my hours and it was a true dream job. I had worked very hard to get it and keep it. I put in extra hours, travelled around the county and, to be honest, sometimes I put work before my home life!

The job paid great wages and enabled my husband and I to get a mortgage to purchase and renovate a beautiful house and turn it into our dream family home. We had wonderful holidays, managed to save money and were able to treat ourselves occasionally too. Life was great and I for one, totally expected it to stay that way!

I remember rumours starting to circulate around the main offices that jobs were being cut and eventually I watched as members of staff were slowly made redundant. Over a couple of years, more and more redundancies were made and whole teams started to disappear. It was an extremely stressful time for all staff in all departments as no-one knew who was next or when the redundancies would stop. Finally a re-shuffle was made of the organisation, removing certain roles and effectively ensuring everyone had to re-apply for the new roles created.

For a couple of years leading up to this process, my husband and I had been very concerned about what we would do if I was made redundant. We relied on my full time wage to pay the mortgage. How would we cope with a major loss of income and pay the bills? My role was quite specific and right across the country similar people in similar roles were being made redundant too – what else could I do? Who would employ me if our skills were no longer required? I have to be honest and say it was a very stressful time for us all. I had worked since I was 16 and was now in my mid 40's – I had never contemplated being out of work!

The inevitable happened and the re-shuffle meant that there was no longer a role for me in the organisation and I, along with many close colleagues were effectively made redundant.

I remember at the time feeling so low, so stressed, so worried about the future that I struggled with my thoughts about how to move forward… what would we do, how will we manage? I could see nothing positive about the future at that particular time. The redundancy money would help us to continue to pay the mortgage and the bills for a few months, but then what? It was a time of blind panic for me and I could see no way out. My job role, the skills and knowledge I had gained over a decade and more, had simply gone. There were no other roles in our geographical area that were anything like the one I had. My role, one that was replicated across the country had, effectively, disappeared.

It wasn't long before we were having money issues and my husband and I sat down with the children and chatted about how we could cut outgoings and costs. We literally made a list of all our outgoings and cut out everything that we could do without from gym membership to satellite TV. We sold things that we didn't need including our beloved campervan. This at least helped pay the mortgage for a few more months and cut down the monthly bills. We ate as cheaply as we could, swapping named brands for cheaper versions. But still I found I was in a very negative space with it all and wanted a solution. I needed something positive to focus on and I needed it now.

I remember clearly my husband and I sitting down round the dining table with a massive piece of flip chart paper and brightly coloured pens with the intention of writing down anything and everything we could think of to get us out of our current situation. We knew we had to do something!

We started to write down what we 'wanted' out of life – we chose deliberately to avoid writing down what we 'did not want' out of life. Only positive things were allowed to be included in our thinking. The first thing we wrote down was our long-term dream which was to retire on a smallholding in Wales. We thought we'd include it in our thinking so we could ensure we spent the next few years working towards it as our ultimate goal. So there it went, in the middle of this flip chart in bright red writing 'Smallholding in Wales'. Our aim was to work out what we would do in the years moving forward from now to get to that goal. We literally sat staring at this large sheet of paper for what seemed like ages.

In a moment of genius we looked at one another and said, 'why not do this now, bring it forward instead of waiting until retirement age!' It was like a positive lightbulb went on in our heads. We couldn't stay as we were, or where we were. We knew we had to sell the house as we could not afford to keep it. We needed to find the positive side of this negative situation.

Why not make our **dream** come true, and why not now!

From that moment on, we chose to seize the opportunity to start something fresh, bring back into play something we had only ever dreamed of doing and turn it into a positive new direction.

We filled that flip chart sheet with positive ideas in bright colours, we discussed what we both wanted, we thought big, we aimed high and we chose not to look back only forward and to make this really happen. We visualised our new home, surrounded by fields, woodlands, sheep, ducks, chickens, pigs, a dog, vegetable patch, even down to the driveway and barns! We planned a business venture that my husband could run from home. One that would pay the bills and would help us back on our feet again. We started to feel excited, we planned so much detail, making lists and notes everywhere – we just knew that this could work and work well too. I even cut out pictures from magazines and images from the internet and made a 'vision board' with everything on it that we **wanted**!

I am so glad we did, I look back now and that old saying "every cloud has a silver lining" comes to mind. My redundancy is never now looked at as a negative, I don't feel negative about it in any way – I see it as a positive. We used those negative emotions, thoughts and feelings and chose to put a stop to them and turn things around.

If I had not been made redundant, I wouldn't be living on my **beautiful** smallholding now! I have acres of fields around me, a stress free lifestyle, no long commutes to work, chickens, ducks, sheep and pigs too. We have a large vegetable garden and I have even planted an orchard! My husband has built up a successful business from home, he loves being here and has the freedom to work for himself too. I even have that perfect dog that I always dreamed of.
I am so glad that I didn't allow those negative thoughts and feelings to bring me down – it's taught me to remember that yes, bad situations do happen. However whenever they arise now I always stop myself and check my thinking and see how I can turn things around looking for the best outcome, the best solution and, for me, it's always going to be a positive one!

Having constant thoughts about money and that you don't have enough makes you stressed, worried and concerned. This brings on negative thoughts and emotions and before you know it money has become this negative monster that brings you down, leaves you feeling distraught and even unwell.

*This is when you need to 'STOP' this way of thinking - remember you are attracting the thought that you don't have enough, you are visualising your life without money and this will attract more of these thoughts. Apply The 'So What!' Theory and START looking at what you do have - a roof over your head, water in the tap, food in the cupboard, see - you are wealthy already! Start attracting money to you - think about what it was like when you last received money – how did you feel? Bet you felt great! Feel it now, imagine yourself receiving money daily, your bank balance growing and **believe** you have enough. Remember like attracts like, so the more positive thoughts and emotions you attach to money, the more positive it becomes. Step out of that negative downward spiral attached to your thoughts and by applying The 'So What!' Theory you can really turn your previous money worries around.*

"Don't just think on the bright side, live on the bright side" M L Holder THE 'SO WHAT!' THEORY

Example 3.

I lost a close member of my family a few years ago and I have to be honest it left me completely devastated. I was totally distraught. My mind was occupied by the loss I felt, the grief, the hole that had opened up in my life where they used to fit. I felt as though part of me was missing and that part would never be replaced. I knew everyone else around me was suffering too, feeling the same way and we clung to each other for comfort as you do when something like this happens. I actually started to feel ill and noticed how it affected my health so quickly. I was feeling very stressed at the time and I am certain this wasn't helping. I knew deep down that given time I would hopefully feel better, but couldn't seem to stop this constant feeling of loss, I was just so sad all the time.

A few weeks passed by and I realised that only I could snap myself out of this 'fog' of grief. I was aware that everyone dealt with their grief differently and ultimately knew I had to deal with mine before it spiralled. I started with small steps. I would get photos out to remind me of this wonderful person, I started to remind myself of when the photo was taken, what we were doing at the time. I started to remember the good times we had, the fun and the laughter. The places we went, the moments that only we shared together. I thought about the things they said to me, the amazing relationship we had and the love and caring we shared. I started to feel better, my memories became emotional and I started to attach positive thoughts to this much loved person in my life. I look back now and am so **glad** that I managed to halt the barrage of negative emotions I was feeling and thinking because when I think of this person today, I smile, I laugh and I remind myself how blessed I am to have had such a wonderful person in my life.

*Death and the loss of someone close, is naturally a difficult time in anyone's life. Dealing with grief, the feeling of loss as well as the stress and worry is a normal human reaction, as is the sadness it can bring. We all deal with grief differently and for some it lasts longer than others. Give yourself time. It is true, time is a healer. Then, when you are ready, apply The 'So What!' Theory. Start to remember the good times, the memories you made together, the positive feelings you had about this person, the fun, the laughter and the experiences shared. Feel blessed that you had this person in your life and start to **celebrate** their life. Attach positive feelings to your thoughts about this* *person so that whenever you think of them you smile and feel happy – it really does help!*

"Live life, love life, be happy" M L Holder
THE 'SO WHAT!' THEORY

Example 4.

I could scream at the amount of times I've tried to help a particular person! All they ever do is moan – this isn't right, that isn't right, the list of things they complain and moan about is literally endless. They are constantly talking about their 'issues' whether it is about work, money, their home, their car, their family. I think we all know this type of person, they have nothing but negative things to say! According to them their life is a misery and whatever solution you provide to their problem there is always a negative answer – 'that won't work because' 'well I've tried this and tried that and it doesn't help' 'no-one understands me' and best of all 'why is my life like this'!! Seriously, I can't remember the last time I ever heard this person say 'I like, or I love'! They really seem to think that their life is the worst in the world.

There have been so many times when I have been brought down by their negative outlook, it smothers you like a blanket and tries to drag you in to that dark mood. It got so bad that I actually started to avoid this person as much as I could and whenever I could. In the end I was attaching negative thoughts, emotions, and feelings to this person so much so, I felt like I was being dragged into this person's negative way of thinking.

So, I decided to tackle this person differently – I had to, otherwise I just couldn't cope with them! Whenever I knew I was going to see this person, I imagined myself with a cloak of protection on so that I wouldn't be able to 'soak' up their negative vibes. I chose not to ask them how they were when we met – I realised I was unwittingly opening the flood gates to their issues by asking each time we met! I consciously steered the conversation on to more positive subjects and pointed out the good things in their life. I smiled a lot in their presence and kept up a positive attitude. Don't get me wrong, it was hard and there were a number of times when I had to pull the conversations around. In the end, I realised that I may not be able to change the way this person views their life. After all it's their choice, their thoughts, feelings and emotions, not mine! But what I was able to do was to change the way I behaved around them, the way I reacted to their moans, complaints and issues. I was conscious that I was not going to agree with their thinking and add fuel to the already well-lit fire. Instead I avoided these types of conversations and focused on the **positives**. I can only hope that by continuing this way with this person that at least I can't be dragged into their world of negativity, I certainly feel better about our meetings!

*We can all think of someone who behaves in this way – someone who feels the world owes them a favour. Someone who feels that their life is nothing but misery! These people are the **perfect example** of how thoughts are energy and how the universal law of attraction works – the more they feel and think negative thoughts and situations, the more they attract it to themselves. They weave a web of negativity around them and, as such, catch more and more negative energy and thoughts. Some even spend their whole lives like this, full of anger and pessimism. Like the turning of a magnet, they repel people away from them. The energy around them feels so negative that you can often feel it when you walk into a room they are in. Nothing ever good happens in these people's lives because they continue to attract bad experiences and situations. They need to break the cycle, and to do this they need to apply The 'So What!' Theory. Even if someone just has a bad start to the day, things can be changed around. They need to stop the negative thinking process and applying positive vibes, energy and thought to change the way the rest of the day plays out.*

If you are close to someone who continually thinks negatively help to remind them what they do have that's good in life. Get them to make a list of the positives around them. This can be the simplest of things – do they have clothes to wear, food in the fridge, money in their wallet. Do they have fresh water in the tap, do they have a home with the comforts that this brings. Remind them that they are **lucky**, *they are blessed to have these things – there are so many people around this world that have absolutely nothing at all. It sounds quite harsh to do this, but stop to think for a moment. Think about what you have yourself, how lucky you are too - these are all positives in life and by helping these constant negative thinkers to apply The 'So What!' Theory to their own lives - even if it's little by little, it will help them to change their views of their own life. It will help them to see the positives in their own lives. After all "small steps are all it takes to start a journey". Tell them - "Change the way you think today and change your life forever……*

"Sprinkle your life with happiness, then share your 'happy glitter' with everyone" M L Holder THE 'SO WHAT!' THEORY

Example 5.

Lying inside an MRI scanner with my head inside a plastic cage, I started to wonder how I had even got here! My thinking was foggy and the noise from the machine wasn't helping as it was incredibly loud. I could remember driving the car then experiencing this excruciating pain in my head. It felt like my head was about to blow open at the crown. I'm still not sure if I actually passed out at the time or not, but by the time I'd come to my senses, I realised I had managed to pull off the road. I felt sleepy, couldn't swallow properly and really wasn't sure what had just happened. How I drove the two miles home I will never know. I do remember my daughter being in the back of the car with me, strapped into her child seat. I remember too, my son greeting me in the driveway and cheekily squirting the car with a water pistol whilst I just sat there, staring at him through the glass side window.

Thankfully by the time my husband tried to get me out of the car he realised very quickly that I had suffered some kind of stroke. I couldn't walk straight, my face felt strange, I was unable to talk properly and I still couldn't swallow properly. It felt like I was about to choke all the time. My mind was very fluffy but I do recall feeling quite upset about not being able to swallow properly.

Ending up in A & E was inevitable, thanks to my husband's quick actions – I just wanted to lie down and go to sleep! The hospital staff were great and suspected a stroke immediately. They acted swiftly to get a CT scan completed, some blood tests and physical tests too. They even performed a lumbar puncture into my spine in case it was meningitis. I was very confused and had no idea what was happening to me, or what was going on around me. Eventually they confirmed it was a Stroke and I spent a week on the stroke ward whilst the staff treated me and assessed my case. I was extremely lucky as my stroke wasn't severe but it had left me without a reaction in the base of my left foot and a brain fog that remained for a number of months! There were a few things about myself that I found were different – I couldn't walk in a straight line properly, I couldn't read properly, I couldn't count or do simple mathematics. I was weaker on my left side, I had lost some feeling in my left arm and If you'd have stuck a sharp needle in the base of my left foot I wouldn't have flinched! I sat around all day in a daze. My husband did absolutely everything for me from feeding me to washing me. He managed the children perfectly – getting them to school, sorting their meals and all the things I had previously done for them. I was off work, felt pretty useless, and started to have feelings of hopelessness about the future. I wanted to be back to normal and get back to my old life. Weeks went by with little improvement apart from some of the brain fog lifting a little.

The GP had been honest and said that the brain sometimes needs its own healing time after a stroke and it's normal to feel 'foggy'. This I could accept but I was starting to get concerned about the rest of my issues. I remember clearly my husband taking my hands in his about 8 weeks after the stroke. He told me that the nurses at the hospital had told him that it was important to rehabilitate as much as you can in the first year because after that, the way you are, is pretty much how you'll be forever. This was news to me! He looked me clear in the eyes and asked me if this was how I wanted to be forever!! I knew this was far from how I wanted to be and an internal panic set in and I just knew I had to do something – anything to improve my situation before it was too late.

The kids got involved – they sat with me at the kitchen table and gave me their school workbooks. There was one called 'mental arithmetic' and it had drawings, writing and numbers which were basically sums to be completed by the reader. I remember my first attempt, it was a series of pictures of coins like 2p + 2p + 1p =? All I had to do was write the answer in the box next to the sum! Half an hour later I had not been able to complete this simple sum, all I had managed to do was write the word 'help!' in pencil next to it. It was at this point I realised this was going to be a massive uphill struggle. I was ready to give everything I had, dig deep and try anything to get myself back to as normal as I possibly could.

The next few months were spent learning to count again, reading as much as I could and attempting to quicken my thinking. It was all in there, I just had to find it again! It was frustrating at times, incredibly hard work and felt like I was climbing my own personal Mount Everest. The more I did, the more I was determined to improve. I joined a gym to try and strengthen my left side of my body – my grip was weak and if I got onto the walking machine, I would naturally head off to the left. Thank goodness it had side bars which stopped me falling off every few seconds! I learnt to use my left arm in a slightly different way as I noticed I kept burning it often without realising – I guess my nerve sensors to the brain had changed!!

Six months on and the difference was **amazing**, my brain was operating so much faster, all the work at the gym had paid off and I could walk normally again. By the time a year had passed I was almost back to normal – almost! I still had 'foggy' brain moments, said words back to front, put things in the wrong places. Physically I still had issues with recognising certain nerves in my left arm and you could still stick a sharp object into the sole of my left foot and I wouldn't flinch. But that was okay – with grit and **determination** I was going to do everything I positively could to be the best I could be after the stroke. Not just for me, but for my children and my husband too – they had gone through this awful journey with me and I felt I owed it to them to be the **best** I could.

I remember holding on to the thought that I was 'lucky', I had a supportive family around me and that there were people all around the world in a far worse situation than I was. The issues I felt were insurmountable at the beginning of my stroke journey, but in reality, they were very small compared to what others went through.

I am now, years on, in the same physical position I was after a year the stroke and that's ok with me. I feel extremely lucky to have been able to push through this ordeal and just so glad I did not give up at any time on that journey. Re-learning from scratch simple things like learning to count is quite a struggle, but it gave me a renewed outlook on my own learning. So much so, that I have continued my learning as an adult since the stroke and even managed to **gain** a degree!

*When major situations arise in life, they can have a huge impact on you and the people around you. They can easily bring your thinking down to a very negative level, after all, they can be life-changing situations and events. At these times it can be incredibly hard to focus on anything positive. This is when positivity is needed at its most – when self-belief and a 'can-do' attitude are what will get you through. This example shows that by breaking the situation down into smaller areas, each one can be tackled, small steps taken lead to larger jumps forward. Each milestone passed is closer to the goal. Whatever the situation, allow that voice inside yourself to say "Don't ever give up- keep going, you can do this!" Apply The 'So What!' Theory and "step over life's hurdles, large or small – then realign your thinking to the positive, whilst striding down your own road of **success**".*

"Yesterday has happened, today is now – so make the most of it" M L Holder THE 'SO WHAT!' THEORY

Example 6.

Stressing myself over the fact that I was running late for another meeting had become a common daily occurrence. My job role meant I had to travel around various parts of the county and meet with people at different times of the day. I was constantly battling with huge volumes of traffic, sitting in traffic jams and praying to the 'traffic light god' to give me green lights all the way! I clearly wasn't praying hard enough for not only did I arrive at the traffic lights as they turned red but I would get stuck at so many! Starting my day across the county had me stressed out before I even started the journey. I would flit between meetings and some days just it felt like it was one bad journey after another. Sometimes it would feel as though my day started off bad and just got worse as it went on. I would be pulled over in some car park between meetings trying to eat a packed lunch and be stressing so much I often spilt food down my suit. Once I even spilt strawberry yoghurt all down my skirt whilst wedged behind the steering when in a parking space of a supermarket and I'd only parked there so I could use their toilet facilities! I was rushed off my feet and arrived at meetings flustered and stressed then have to leave in a hurry for the next meeting. I lost count of the times I complained to anyone and everyone that 'my day just couldn't have been any worse'. I would arrive home exhausted and wish that I'd had a better day.

This went on week after week and I realised I was making myself stressed and unhappy and experiencing negative feelings and thoughts about my job and essentially, I'd had enough. I sat down one Saturday morning and went back through my past few weeks in my head. It wasn't long before I realised it wasn't the job I was negative about, it was the way I approached it. I was making myself stressed. I was starting my day stressed and feeling bad about the day before it actually happened! I decided to put a plan into practise whereby I would not only schedule my meetings more effectively but allow ample travelling time between each one and ensure I had break points too. Getting from A-B, B-C and C-D could be achieved in a much calmer way avoiding stress. I realised my stress levels went up through the day and by changing the way I approached my day I could avoid this happening as much. The first week after starting my new approach went fairly well, I had to keep reminding myself to stop rushing around so much quite a few times, but I noticed that I had felt better overall at the end of the day. I still managed to get the same amount of work done, however it was in a **calmer** happier way!

*If you are finding that you are having a 'bad' day for whatever reason, avoid adding any more bad or negative thoughts to the rest of the day, otherwise things can seem as though they go from bad to worse! Stop yourself at any point during your day when you feel things are not going in perhaps the way you want them to. Apply The 'So What!' Theory - Think about how you DO want your day to go, what would be a positive outcome and focus on that instead. Don't waste your energy stressing over traffic – you'll arrive at your destination anyway! If you have to be somewhere at a particular time, plan your route in advance, allow time for the journey and add extra if you are worried about traffic. If you're having a run of 'bad' days try visualising your day ahead in a positive way, before it's even started. Either when you go to bed the night before or when you get up in the morning. Take a couple of minutes and try running your day ahead through your own mind and seeing it being a positive, happy, successful day with **amazing** outcomes. Imagine each journey going well, each meeting having great results. Whatever your day ahead whether it be at work, a day at home, visiting friends and family or going shopping – take time to visualise it in a positive way, before it even happens!*

*Even down to the last detail – you can even write it down in advance if you have time! You will be surprised at how much of a difference this will have on your day. It attaches good thoughts, positive emotions and great energy to your day ahead. If your day didn't go as planned, think back to areas of it that you can identify went wrong and plan how you can make changes for the next time you are in the same situation. Before you know it you will not only be having amazingly **productive** and happy days, but weeks and months too!*

"Think about what you do want rather that what you don't" M L Holder THE 'SO WHAT!' THEORY

Example 7.

Finally getting a proper diagnosis was a blessing for me – if that makes sense! For years, in fact right back to childhood, I had suffered with health issues. It was literally the most random selection of ailments that anyone could have. I was experiencing a long list of issues – daily headaches, weekly migraines, serious fatigue, joint pain, muscle aches, mouth and nose ulcers, dry eyes, unexplained bruising and skin rashes. I had episodes when my chest was so painful when I breathed and other times when it felt like my heart was beating erratically! I had sadly suffered a couple of miscarriages and at one point was told I might be unable to have children. My list of health issues was getting longer and more complicated and despite various treatments for differing things over the years, I knew that something still wasn't quite right but was unable to figure out what.

All of my health issues had an impact on my life in some way or another. Raising a family and managing to work full time became, at times, quite challenging. I would never know how I was going to feel from one week to the next and even when I did feel really unwell, I still had to keep going.

I finally got a diagnosis of Antiphospholipid Syndrome (APS), also known as Hughes Syndrome. Named after Professor Hughes, who discovered its existence in the 1980's. As a child of the 60's I realised that I could not have had a proper diagnosis as this illness had not even been discovered back then! APS is an autoimmune disease that affects the blood, causing blood clots in the body (something I had also suffered) as well as pregnancy complications, which explained my infertility issues and miscarriages. Symptoms also included migraines, headaches and heart valve disease. Whilst this diagnosis captured many of my 'random' health issues and meant I could now get the right treatment, it did not explain all of them. Medical professionals that helped me gain this diagnosis, raised the fact that many APS sufferers also had an overlap with other autoimmune diseases. So I had further testing and it was indeed confirmed that I had something called 'Lupus' (Systemic Lupus Erythematous) as well as Sjogren's Disease. In fact, it turned out that the Lupus was the main autoimmune disease and from that, it caused the APS and Sjogren's. It turned out that everything wrong with my health right back to childhood was in fact caused by these autoimmune diseases! Lupus is an autoimmune disease in which the body's immune system mistakenly attacks healthy tissue in the body from the skin, the internal organs to the joints. My body was literally attacking itself day in day out. Sjogren's is an autoimmune disease that attacks the moisture-producing glands of the body, hence the dry eyes and mouth.

I was shocked at my diagnosis, but at the same time not! At least I now understood what had been wrong with me for the past few decades, it explained a lot. I spent the first few weeks after my diagnosis is a sort of haze – none of these immune system issues were curable, they were for life. I soon became aware that historically the average life expectancy of someone with Lupus wasn't great. For some, it was in the past, around 10 years! This worried me greatly – okay I panicked! – I had clearly had this disease already for a very long time, well over 10 years, and with no treatment at all. So what was my life expectancy? The answer to this is unknown, getting the best treatment possible is important, as was getting a baseline idea of how my internal organs were. I went through a multitude of various investigations to check everything from my heart, lungs, brain, kidneys, liver and my joints and bones. Some of these involved different scanning processes such as ultrasound, MRI and CT scans. Some were by x-ray and some were by blood tests.

The results revealed a multitude of issues including damage already done to some internal organs such as my heart and brain. I had connective tissue disease, hypermobility, borderline osteoporosis and Raynaud's disease to add to the mix. However, all of this at least explained why I had felt so ill for years – I finally felt as though I had gained a thorough overview of what was happening to me and this meant that treatment could begin to help me. It was a great relief that I now knew what was wrong, I could understand myself better and could explain to those around me what was going on with me.

Treatment for me was going to be lifelong and with there being no cure, I had to hope that my immune system could be suppressed enough to stop it from attacking itself. This is achieved for the most part using immunosuppressants in the form of weekly oral Chemotherapy as well as Steroid treatments. I also take a daily cocktail of medications morning and night and have regular blood tests to check my internal organs and inflammation markers in my body. I have regular scans on my internal organs and see a number of medical consultants on a regular basis to help keep on top of all the issues that these autoimmune diseases cause.

Did I feel upset and angry at what was happening to me – YES! At one point, as more and more diagnoses were revealing themselves, I felt completely overwhelmed and lost for a time. I struggled to understand what was happening to me let alone explain it to anyone else. I knew I had to come to terms with all that had happened in the past and all that would happen in the future. I included my immediate family in discussions about the issues at hand, they were incredibly supportive and understanding.

I researched so much about all these labels now attached to me and in the end I felt quite scared about the future. I was still going to feel the pain associated with much of my illnesses. I would still feel the symptoms that each one brought to the table and I would still need to carry on with my everyday life in the same way I always did. I had no idea how I could achieve this, but made an early decision to make the best of a bad situation. Understanding what all these illnesses were was key to this. I bought as many books as I could get on each of the diagnosed illnesses, researched the internet, joined forums and support groups and contacted any national help groups for each one too. I figured out that if I personally knew all there was to know about my issues, I could monitor my body and take action if anything wasn't right. If my chest became particularly painful as it often did, I knew it was pleurisy and visited the GP. If my kidneys played up which was common for me, I again headed to the GP for treatment. I quickly realised that I needed to understand how my body felt and how to help it in the best way I could. It was clear that these autoimmune issues could not be ignored in anyway if I was to have any chance of a future. I pictured my immune system as an army. When I felt okay, I imagined my army on leave, when I was having a full blown flare, my army was in attack.

My determination to get as much quality and quantity out of my life became important to me and I started to focus on the positive attitude that this required. Keeping on top of everything, with the support of the medical professionals around me was my challenge. Not only that, it was the key to my future. It's obvious that these illnesses have a huge effect on how I live my life and what I can and can't do on a daily basis. My treatments have changed over the past few years as my immune system has sadly become more and more active. The need for stronger immunosuppressant treatment has increased and the weekly chemotherapy levels have increased to cope with that.

Looking to the future is uncertain, and at times scary. However I made a decision a few months after my diagnosis to do everything in my **power** to push through all of this and to focus on staying as positive as I can. I felt that if I was negative, it would depress me, upset me, and ultimately made me feel worse. This had an effect on my health. I found it was easy to spiral downwards and I really didn't, at any time, want to feel sorry for myself. I kept the view that this has happened, it is happening, and I can't stop it, change it or take it away, so I'd better find a way of dealing with it. I also found that if I was negative about my situation, it affected those around me too and I really didn't want my family feeling sad about my health issues. I wanted them to support me in visualising a **bright** future and they wouldn't be able to do this if I wasn't bright about it too.

I was glad I now had treatment, grateful I had medications to help me, and a supportive network of healthcare professionals working with me for the best positive outcome available to me. I refused to curl up on the sofa, feel sorry for myself and give up. Worrying about what the future would bring was pointless and caused stress, so why bother! I knew I was unable to do certain things as and when I wanted to, however I did everything I could to focus on what I was able to do and to take every **opportunity** that came my way.

*When times are tough and you are faced with a situation that seems all consuming, try to find something positive to focus on – think about what you 'can' do rather than what you 'can't'. Find that something positive, hold onto it, then find another and keep going – you will find more! Keep on trying no matter what and regardless of how tough it can get. Make every day the best it can be. It is all too easy to take the alternative route and to give up, spend every day in bed, feel sorry for yourself, curl up on the sofa, complain to everyone, post on social media daily about how awful your life is. What does this achieve – absolutely nothing! All it does is put you in a negative frame of mind and keep you there, wallowing in self-pity and attracting more and more negative thoughts and as such more negative issues to you. Don't worry and stress about what's to come. Don't restrict yourself from doing what you want to do. Push past it all, think positive, think "I can", "**I will**", "I want to...so I shall". Use positive language wherever you can, even when times are at their toughest find something positive to make you smile. Involve those close to you, ask them to help you find positive things to talk* *about including good solutions to your situation. Think about a positive future and visualise what this will look like. Feel it emotionally and hold onto that feeling. Remember to focus on what you do want, not what you don't want. Above all remember your thoughts are energy and act like a magnet – what you put out, you will* **attract** *back!*

"Let the sea of positivity wash over you and cleanse you of any negative thoughts" M L Holder THE 'SO WHAT!' THEORY

Example 8.

I think the most difficult time in my life was when it was made clear to me that I had a very slim chance of survival. I was in an isolation unit in intensive care and to be honest, I felt so ill, I wasn't sure myself if I actually wanted to live. It literally was that bad for me.

Having taken some medication for a newly diagnosed health issue, I was suffering with a severe reaction to this particular medication. It started with a rash and ended up with me nearly losing my life. I had been seen by various nurses and doctors at my local GP Practise and had even been sent to the Accident and Emergency department, as they had realised what was happening to me. Unfortunately for me, despite being taken directly to the acute medical unit where I was examined then bandaged back up, the decision was made to send me home! I was desperate to be treated for this reaction and was utterly shocked that they had decided to send me home. I think they had no idea what to do with me – they said I was at risk of infection as my body was an open wound, therefore in their opinion I would be safer off at home. So, a few days later, having been rushed back to hospital in a state of complete dehydration and with my body a burnt mess, it was no surprise that the medical staff struggled numerous times to find a vein somewhere. They tried everywhere on my body that they could insert a cannula into. Without this there could be no treatment for me. I was made aware that even with treatment, the reaction would only stop raging through my body when it wanted to, regardless of any treatment.

The rash developed quickly, covered my entire body, then blistered and left me losing layer after layer of my skin. The reaction affected 98% of my skin. My medication had caused a rare but severe reaction known as Stevens-Johnson syndrome (SJS). This reaction causes your body to effectively burn itself from the inside out. It works its way through your internal organs and anything and everything inside you, until it reaches your outer layer which is your skin. It burns your skin leaving you with 2nd and 3rd degree burns. If you have more than 30% coverage on your body, it turns into something called Toxic Epidermal Necrolysis and your skin dies and completely peels off in layers in the areas affected. For me, the only area unaffected was the top of my scalp, the rest of me was a burnt mess. As if this wasn't enough to deal with, all my mucous membranes had burnt, so I produced no saliva, tears etc.

My eyeballs were burning too. Add to this the fact that by the time I got into intensive care my veins had all collapsed, it soon became clear that treating me was going to be an issue. At this point, I was pretty much ready to just give up as I was so exhausted from the pain. I had been unable to move for a couple of weeks as my skin was continuously blistering and weeping and was unbearably painful and sore. My internal organs screamed at me and my muscles and joints were swollen and extremely painful.

I thought my luck had turned when, with the use of an ultrasound machine and me pinned to the operating table, the surgeon managed to get the cannula into a vein in my neck. From this, they could take blood to check on my internal organs and pump me full of a concoction of medication through various drips. Sadly I thought wrong – lying in intensive care, the SJS got worse for the next three days. It clearly wasn't ready to leave my body just yet. My head started to swell up, it literally puffed up like a balloon with my eyes so swollen I couldn't open them for a while. All this time my skin continued to come off in sheets. The nurses tended to me 24 hours a day – removing layers of my skin, covering me with emollient from head to toe and then re-bandaging me. I was a massive open wound and a serious infection risk. I had times when I remember thinking 'just let it be all over' the pain was indescribable. There was nowhere on my body that didn't hurt and hurt badly. Everyone who entered my isolation room on the intensive care unit for the first time, looked shocked at my appearance. I clearly looked like a burnt mess. Luckily for me there were no mirrors, nor could I have stood to look into one! Having a cannula in my neck was a success and they started treating me with Intravenous Immunoglobulin (IVIG). This treatment contains the pooled immunoglobulin G (IgG) which are immunoglobulins from the plasma of approximately a thousand or more blood donors per bag, and I went through bags of it.

A few days later saw a turning point and the swelling on my head started to recede. The morphine pain relief that was being fed to me through a drip was finally helping me to cope with some of the pain. The IVIG that they had been treating me with was working and my body started to make the very long journey that would be my healing process. I spent a while in the intensive care unit having constant treatment for my burns and stayed there until I was more stable and out of danger. I was then moved into another isolation unit in another part of the hospital whilst I recovered further. Most sufferers of this awful reaction are treated in a burns unit and put into an induced coma. Unfortunately for me, it was too dangerous to move me to another hospital. I seriously believe that if I had been put into a coma, I would not be here to tell the tale.

Even today, I still suffer with the fall out that this reaction causes. Your body is never the same again. I had very nasty scars as a result of the burns, my internal organs suffered as did my eyes. I struggled to produce saliva and was unable to sweat or cry. Your body literally dries up as all of the mucous membranes are burnt away. It's incredibly challenging and quite painful to eat food without saliva or to cry without tears! SJS and TENs is seen as a massive immune system failure, so that in itself leaves you with lifelong health issues.

Despite everything I was going through during this torturous time for me, I had made a pact with myself. If the hospital staff could get a cannula into my body (they had tried many times in multiple places with ultrasound, all unsuccessfully), then I was going to fight this awful reaction mentally and with all my will power. I was determined that no matter how slim my chances were, I was going to fight this and survive to tell the tale. Even at the very worst – I remember the date, it was 3rd February 2011, and I still maintained a positive outlook and state of mind. I had so much to fight for – and so much life yet to live that I was not going to give up and if I was to die, I would at least die fighting! I held onto that positive frame of mind right through my slow recovery – and it was seriously slow. I had good days and bad days and even when my body was starting to heal, I found my emotions were all over the place. Despite this, I always focused on the end goal – recovery.

I knew that my life would never be the same. This awful reaction would scar my body and mind for ever. However, I was so happy that I had survived! It has been said that this reaction is so rare you have a 1 in 1.3 million chance of getting it. Many, sufferers don't make it through the reaction and die. Many are left blind or seriously visually impaired. All will have lifelong health issues. I am lucky to have support from other sufferers around the world and have actually now met three survivors in the UK and been in touch with people from as far away as India, Australia and America. My eyes are in a fairly good condition, I do have a few issues with them but it's nothing compared to some of the other survivors. I have some nerve damage in my brain, some heart damage, severely dry eyes and mouth, skin scars, digestion issues, daily headaches and a host of other issues far too long to list here. However, I did it – I kept a positive mental attitude throughout and in my head I fought this awful reaction with everything I had. I was determined to survive at all costs. My family were positive too and helped me to stay positive and I know this helped. I tried not to worry as I just knew I had to survive this.

Yes, it changed my life – it put into perspective how important things are in life to me. It reminded me that not one day should be wasted. It reminded me that leading a positive way of life with a more positive outlook and frame of mind, was the only way forward. I was mindful that others had not survived this reaction and those that did, had some seriously horrendous health issues, many worse than mine. I reminded myself that people all over this world have other seriously major health issues or disabilities, and many of them were in a far worse situation than I was. I also said to myself 'ok, this has happened, 'so what'…let's get over it and move on! I was so very grateful for the bags of IVIG that I was given and to the thousands and thousands of people that donated their blood so I could survive. The dedicated medical staff that treated me continuously throughout this ordeal – I trusted them with my life and they remained positive and driven throughout. I was **lucky** to have my family and friends around me. The unfaltering support from my husband who spent every day with me, encouraging me and keeping me positive. My beautiful children who despite their own upset and worry, fought my corner, supported and **encouraged** me to get better. My parents, sisters, brother-in-law and extended family... they all helped to me through this and supported me through my long recovery. Without my positive mental attitude and pure determination to survive, this story would have had a very different ending.

This example shows that no matter how traumatic an experience is at the time you are going through it, there is always something positive you can try to find and focus on to help you through. Even if it is after the event or situation that you try to find something positive, it's a start. Sometimes things in life are so huge and life changing that we often feel unable to look to the positive side of things. But if we are to move forward, to keep going, to get back on track, then we must look for the positive - we must have hope for the future. Remind yourself *that you can 'do this', you can adopt a positive mental attitude and you can succeed. Some of the most challenging things we go through in life can make us stronger. If you find yourself thinking negative thoughts, remember to apply The 'So What!' Theory and change your thoughts to positive ones. Tell yourself that there are people around this world in a far worse situation than yours. Seek support from others if and when you need it. Don't feel alone in your thoughts, often it helps to discuss a problem or concern and share it with someone you trust. Focus on how you want your future to be, focus on your recovery, your life-goals and keep hold of these as they will always **spur** you on.*

"Focus on your future, not your past" M L Holder THE 'SO WHAT!' THEORY

These examples are not a collection of people's lives. They are my life. Each one of these stories I have lived, experienced and now told.
All of them may seem negative to start with, but each and every one of them shows how, if you let positive thinking creep in bit by bit that you **can** help yourself through any situation no matter how bad or difficult it is. You may not be able to take away your issues, but you can

certainly help yourself to get through your life in a more positive and happy way! Refer to the 'Self Help' section in this book for ways to keep your thinking as positive as it can be even in the most difficult of times.

6 EXERCISES

In this section there are some exercises to try, particularly if there is a specific area of life or a situation that you are unhappy about. This can be applied to anything large or small, complex or simple, and at any time.

- Write down what the issue, situation or thinking is, that you want to change. Using a piece of paper, make a list. Be honest with yourself, explore all your feelings and get it all down on paper. Then put this to one side.

- Using another piece of paper, start to think about what you do want from this issue/situation or thought. What result do you want? What solution are you after? What would be the very **best** outcome for you? If it helps, write it all down and use positive words where you can. Try using bright coloured pens or paper, post-it notes, bold letters – whatever helps you to visualise the best. Include how this brilliant result will make you feel, what it will achieve, how it will make you think. List the emotions it evokes. How will this great solution to your issue look when it's as perfect as it can be? Use bullet points if they help, or numbers – whatever makes this exercise easiest for you. Start thinking 'how am I going to change this' 'what am I going to do first' then start listing it. Get excited about this new list – it's going to be your plan to use The 'So What!' Theory and say 'So What!' – 'I **can** change this around' I **can** move forward to a positive solution and outcome. 'I really **can** do this'. By the end of the exercise you will have a plan of action, one that helps you to change your thinking and feeling about the situation you started off with. You now have a positive way forward! Try it now – think of something in your life that you want to change for the better and give it a go. You will be surprised at how easy it is!

- Now compare the two lists, note how they make you feel. Notice that you feel better reading the positive list – it evokes **better** energy, better feelings and a better outcome.

- Now throw away the negative list, the one that shows the current situation. You don't need this anymore – from now on you are going to only focus on the positive outcomes! Imagine what it would feel like to have a successful outcome, evoke the emotions within yourself. Hold onto those feelings and store them in your brain so you can tap into them at any time.

- Keep the positive list - it shows you how you can change the situation around. Make as many lists as you need for each issue, concern or area of negativity in your life. These lists are your route to a **successful** outcome.

Use this exercise simply and quickly anywhere at any time. The more you try it the easier and quicker it becomes. I've used it effectively at work, at home and have even on occasion, surpassed the need for paper lists. If it's a simple issue you can even go through the issue in your mind and break it down – thinking about how you can **change** it simply and quickly into a positive.

Remember to apply The 'So What!' Theory to any situation – just make yourself STOP the way you are thinking and **START** to think about how you can change it for a positive outcome.

"Your thoughts are free – make them all good ones" M L Holder THE 'SO WHAT!' THEORY
Gratitude Exercises

This exercise will help you to show your thanks and **gratitude** for anything and everything in your life! To start with, and to make this exercise simple for your first time of trying it, think of three things that you are grateful for in your life. If you find this hard to do then you can use some ideas from the list of suggestions below.

- Home
- Car
- Job
- Food
- Clothes
- Family
- Electronic gadgets
- Friendships

Once you have chosen the three things you are grateful for – list each of them, then start to think about why you are grateful for them. How do they affect your life in a positive way? What do they help you to **achieve**? Take time to focus on each thing you've chosen. List as much as you can think of including all the processes or the journey that the item may have made to get to you.

Try to make time to do this exercise as often as possible, daily if you can. Very soon you will find yourself offering thanks for things as they happen. You can take your gratitude to a higher level – I often give thanks for things before I actually purchase them or ask the universe for them! I give thanks every time money comes to me. You can try this too. It is particularly **helpful** if you have issues around money and have, in the past, attached negative thoughts and emotions to finances. Remember you are a thought magnet and so you need to think good and positive thoughts to attract the same back to you! Whenever money comes to you, as a gift or as wages or from something you sell – show your gratitude and **attract** more. Imagine every time you open your front door there is money sitting there waiting for you. Or someone has sent you money in the post. How great would that feel!

Doing this exercise is good for you, it helps to remind you of the **great** things you have in your life already. It helps you to think about how these items came to you and the people that helped in that process. It gives us all a way of recognising how lucky we already are and that there are so many positive things in our lives that we can focus on. It attaches positive energy to our thinking and as such it attracts more of the **good** things in our lives to us. Even better – it costs us nothing to do this exercise, just a little moment of our time to offer thanks for what we have.

"Share your good fortunes and inspire others to achieve" M L Holder THE 'SO WHAT!' THEORY

7 SELF HELP

The 'So What!' Theory Self Help guide to being positive.

This section includes some 'self-help' steps to keeping positive. You can use these daily or simply whenever you feel the need for a positive **boost**!

Firstly, take some time to evaluate your thinking processes – what do you focus on the most, is it positive or negative thoughts? Are you constantly focusing or talking about what you don't want? Many of us find that we are almost programmed to think and worry about negative things and we often fall victim to giving these types of thoughts all our energy. We complain and moan that things aren't going well and subconsciously move on. Rarely do we stop to see how we could have made a situation better!

"You may not be able to prevent things and situations from happening to you. You can, however, do something about how you

react and feel about it" M L Holder THE 'SO WHAT!' THEORY

Step 1.
Spend time writing down specific areas of your life that you are currently unhappy about or that are particularly negative. Write as much as you need to – get it all down on paper or if it helps, type it up. This process will help you to really take a good look at your current situation and identify what it is that isn't working well for you and why. This can often be quite cathartic and will no doubt, evoke some powerful emotions in you. This is because our emotions are attached to our thoughts. This first exercise will help you to move forward from a negative view on these areas of your life to a more positive and **happy** one. Remember, The 'So What!' Theory aims to help you make changes to your thinking so that these areas of your life that you currently view as unhappy or negative will become positive. Not only that, but you will be able to turn them into happy, satisfied areas of your life. Doing these exercises will enable you to tackle each and every one of the areas of your life that you want to and can change.

"Good thoughts are like trees, plant them well and watch them flourish" M L Holder
THE 'SO WHAT!' THEORY

Step 2.
From what you have written in step 1, make a list of what it is that you want to change right now. You can tackle these one at a time or spend longer and choose to **evaluate** more.

Step 3.
Once you have your list, take each issue and start to think how you'd like things to be. Take as much time as you need and really evaluate things – if it helps, **visualise** how you'd like a situation to be. By now you will know what you don't want, so start to focus on what you do want.

Step 4.
Now that you have had a chance to think about how you do want each issue or area of your life to be, write down how it **will** be. Use emotions and positive language, for example. *"I have money in my purse and in the bank and I will attract more money to me. I am so lucky to have this money and every day I give thanks for it"*. Or *"Today is going to be a great day at*

work, I will achieve everything I need to and on time. I will really enjoy my day – thank you!" It is important not to just write it down but to also **imagine** how this will feel when it has happened. Ask yourself how will you feel when you attract lots of money or have a fabulous day at work? Stop now and think about it!

Remember that Step 4 can be applied to any situation, anytime and anywhere. Once you have practised this a few times on paper you will be able to do this in your head! You can literally be sitting on a train, in a car, in a conference, in a restaurant or at home. You'll soon be applying this exercise easily and quickly to enable you to evaluate any negative situation and to apply The 'So What!' Theory to STOP any bad thoughts arising. It really is that simple! Apply Step 3 to think about how you do want this situation to be for the **better**, think of a positive solution, turn things around and apply Step 4. Before you know it you will be doing this as a daily practise, quickly and effectively with amazing results!

"Be positive, stay positive" M L Holder THE 'SO WHAT!' THEORY

If you feel that you want to take this exercise a step further and to perhaps a whole new level involving every area of your life, start by asking yourself - what are your goals in life? Have you ever taken time to think about what you want out of life? If not, then now is the time to do so – it's good to have a positive outlook on your future and it's great to have something in life to **aim** for! Make a list of your goals. Is it a new job, a chance to travel, a new car, a new home, great friendships or a life-partner? Doing this will help you to reflect on your current life situation and can **spur** you on to great things. You can even make a vision board if it helps by cutting out pictures of what you want in your life. Use images, symbols and positive words and put them together on a page or a board. Stick them on using glue or you can even create a computer generated image board! Once you have done this, place it where you can see it often. Focus on these images, **evoke** the feelings that you will have when these things are in your life and above all remind yourself it is important to be thankful for the things that will be coming to you, so always ensure you show **gratitude** in advance of receiving them.

- Remember you are a magnet and by sending out the thought of wanting these things in your life, you will start to **attract** them more easily.

- Remember to think positively about what you want and to evoke the feelings of happiness and **joy** you will feel when you have them.

- Keep track of your life **goals**, keep adding new ones and remember to 'think big!'

If you are having a particular bad point during the day here are a few ideas of things to try to help stay positive and to cheer yourself up.

- Play music that you find **uplifting** if you need a 'happy boost' – you will soon find yourself feeling cheerful! Try to avoid songs with negative wording.
- Speak to someone who always makes you feel good – maybe someone you have a special connection with.
- Spend some time with your pet – cuddling an animal evokes happy emotions!
- Go for a walk outside – take yourself away from where you are experiencing the negative thoughts and emotions
- Meditate – think of positive things to focus on, practise mindfulness

- Do some doodling on paper, draw happy faces!
- Tell someone some jokes – make yourself **laugh**!
- Watch a comedy on TV or a fun movie that you like. Choose one that you know will make you feel great!
- Give and receive hugs – they always make you feel **better**!
- Do an activity you know you will enjoy – go to the gym, the movies, cook a meal you **enjoy**, have a long relaxing bath.
- Smile at everyone you see. Go and find someone nearby, say Hi and smile at them.
- Spend time with your **loved** ones, your family, your friends
- Dance – let yourself go and pretend no one's watching!

There are bound to be other things that you can think of that will work well for you. Add them to the list and remember at negative times to apply The 'So What!' Theory, stop your thought patterns and turn things around!

"Love life, it's good for you!" M L Holder
THE 'SO WHAT!' THEORY

If you are finding your days pass by and rather than just having a few negative moments, you feel pretty down about the whole day, then try the following exercise.

Your positive day could look like this……

- Get up every day with a smile on your face. Look in the mirror and tell yourself "today is an **amazing** day and great things will happen"

- Take a moment to run through the day ahead in your mind and visualise everything you have planned from the journey to work, the people you will see, to the shopping you need to do on the way home. Visualise everything you do today as going **fantastically** well! Evoke the feelings associated with success, happiness and joy at your day being perfect. Attach those feelings to your vision of your day ahead. Hold onto those feelings, smile to yourself as you start your perfect day!

- Use positive language as much as you can all day. Use words like I can, I will, this went really well, amazing, it was great when, I loved doing this because…

Try using words from the 'Page of Positivity' in this book, or think of your own **positive** words!

- Try to keep a positive mental attitude throughout your day.

- Smile at everyone you meet even if you don't know them! It's **fun**, it's free and it won't hurt you – so go on, give it a try! You'll be amazed at how good it makes you feel and it will make a difference to your day – and theirs!

- Inject laughter into the day if you can. **Laughter** is infectious and very good for lifting our mood!

- Remind yourself at certain points during the day at how lucky you are to have good things in your life. Think of three random things in your life that you are grateful for and list them. Try drawing a **smiley** face and listing the three things below it. Remember there is always someone out there who is far worse off than you who doesn't have these three things. Repeat this exercise a couple of times a day if you can, even if it's just a mental note of three things! Do this every day and chose different things each day to list.

- If others around you are being negative, try to offer positive solutions in a gentle and calming way. Sometimes it helps us in our own thinking to evaluate how others are thinking about a situation. Can we apply The 'So What!' Theory to their situation? What would we do differently to them right now to change a negative into a positive? It's great to practise this, as it reminds us that everyone **can** change their thinking for the positive!

- If things go 'off track' and negativity creeps in, apply The 'So What!' Theory, change your own thinking and start again… keep up the positivity!

- Practice your gratitude – you can do this as things happen or at the end of the day. Remember this can be done verbally or you can jot the things that you are grateful for in a notebook or on a piece of paper.

- At the end of the day and before you go to sleep – run back through the day you had in your head, and see how positive it was! **Feel** that positivity and the happy emotions it brings. Give thanks for your amazing day and attach positive emotions to tomorrow! If you found that you experienced negative thoughts in some areas of your day, reflect on how it could have gone better, how you could change it for a more positive outcome. Remember that next time this happens you can think differently and avoid the negative and swap for the positive!

- Start the whole process over again the next day

Within a few days you will have had an opportunity to practise this a few times and each day you do this it gets easier. Each and every day you will feel better about yourself and the things you do. Remind yourself that it's okay if an issue or problem arises because it's how you deal with it now that matters. From now on you can look for positive outcomes and **solutions** rather than accepting a negative one.

"Thoughts have no boundaries, so think big!" M L Holder THE 'SO WHAT!' THEORY

Once you have started to think more positively, keep going...send out positivity wherever you go and whatever you are doing remember *"Change the way you think today and change your life forever!"*

Stress

Stress can seriously affect how we feel as it attracts a lot of negative thinking and emotions. Stress can for some, really affect their health and not in a good way. It has been shown that stress can contribute to numerous health issues such as heart disease, high blood pressure and obesity. It can make your heart race, make you feel on edge, make you tearful or even angry. Stress can lead to feelings of sadness, hopefulness and depression. It is a huge subject area and there are many websites dedicated to identifying, recognising and dealing with it. The 'So What!' Theory wants to help the reader to recognise when stress is affecting our mood, our thinking and our behaviour and help to STOP this. It will help you to change the way you are thinking about stress and move to a more positive frame of mind. This will enable you to tackle the issues causing the stress in the first place. Below is a short list of things you can do to try to alleviate your stress.

- The first thing to do is to start to alter your thinking, much in the way this book is helping you to do this already. Try to stop thinking negatively about the stressful situation you are in and try to think positively.

- If you're stressed because you are rushing around doing so much you can't cope, try prioritising your day or tasks. Work out the ones that are important and need completing first. Make a list with the urgent things at the top. This will help you to plan your day **effectively** and it helps to get through that list more easily.

- Assess what specific areas of your life cause the stress triggers. Is it a specific place, situation or time of the day?

- Identify some specific time in the day as 'me time'. It is important to give yourself some quiet thinking space and to forget your worries and **relax**.

- Use methods to help you take your mind off your stresses – listen to music, do exercise, take a walk, meet friends. Anything that you **like** to do that you know de-stresses you.

- If you get particularly stressed at work, be sure to take breaks. Remove yourself from the desk or the building and get some fresh air - take a walk around the building.

- If you are having health issues that you feel are related to stress and are unable to reduce your stress levels yourself, try talking things through with a friend or family member. If things are serious, do seek medical advice.

"Laughter is infectious, spread it everywhere!" M L Holder THE 'SO WHAT!' THEORY

Always remember that the most important thing with self-help is YOU! You **can** change the way you think about situations and issues. You are in control of your own thoughts, emotions and feelings, so make them count – make them **positive**.

Below are a few positive words that you can try to use as often as possible – if it helps write some of them on sticky note pads and place them wherever you can see them. This is particularly helpful if you have specific areas where you may feel particularly negative as it helps you to focus on the positive more easily!

Smile
Wonderful
Yes
Confident
Optimistic
Achieve
Exciting
Brilliant
Perfect
Success
Gratitude
Believe
Happy
Content
Laugh
I will
I can
I am

And finally.......

You've done it! Your first steps to changing your life are complete and you have finished reading the book. The learning and knowledge from this book will carry on forever, and by using these exercises and referring back to this book regularly, you can always ensure that you stay positive.

If you've been through some tough times and managed to see the positive instead of the negative, then share your story and help to inspire others. Send it to me at the website – I'd love to hear from you!

Email – hello@thesowhattheory.com

Website - www.thesowhattheory.com

Listed below are a selection of helpful websites.

The 'So What!' Theory website. This website supports the book and has downloadable copies of the 'page of positivity' and the 'So What!' speech bubbles. The website provides even more inspirational ways to stay positive!
www.thesowhattheory.com

Antiphospholipid Syndrome Support UK
www.aps-support.org.uk

Lupus UK website
www.lupusuk.org.uk

British Sjögren's Syndrome Association
www.bssa.uk.net

Scleroderma & Raynaud's UK
www.sruk.co.uk

Stevens-Johnson Syndrome Awareness UK
www.sjsawareness.org.uk

Hypermobility UK
www.hypermobility.org

Stroke Association UK
www.stroke.org.uk